BOOK 1 - Timpani & Auxiliary

STANDARD OF EXCELLENCE

COMPREHENSIVE BAND METHOD

By Bruce Pearson

Dear Student:

Welcome to the wonderful world of instrumental music. The moment you pick up your drum sticks and mallets, you will begin an exciting adventure that is filled with challenges and rewards. If you study carefully and practice regularly, you will quickly discover the joy and satisfaction of playing beautiful music for yourself, your family, your friends, or a concert audience.

I hope you have many rewarding years of music-making.

Best wishes,

Bruce Pearson

In this book, you will learn to play many different percussion instruments. Use the following list to help you find where each percussion instrument is introduced.

<table>
<tr><td>Claves - p. 19</td><td>Tambourine - p. 11</td></tr>
<tr><td>Crash Cymbals - p. 26</td><td>Timpani - p. 16</td></tr>
<tr><td>Maracas - p. 19</td><td>Triangle - p. 3</td></tr>
<tr><td>Sleigh Bells - p. 9</td><td>Temple Blocks - p. 23</td></tr>
<tr><td>Suspended Cymbal - p. 2</td><td>Wood Block - p. 8</td></tr>
</table>

SPECIAL NOTE: Pages 36-37, 39-40, 42, 46, and 48 are not included in this book. Use the STANDARD OF EXCELLENCE Drums & Mallet Percussion book when the band is playing from these pages.

*The author wishes to thank percussionist **Sam Lutfiyya** for his contributions to this book.*

ISBN 0-8497-5946-3

KJOS NEIL A. KJOS MUSIC COMPANY, PUBLISHER

W21TM

THE SUSPENDED CYMBAL (S. Cym.)

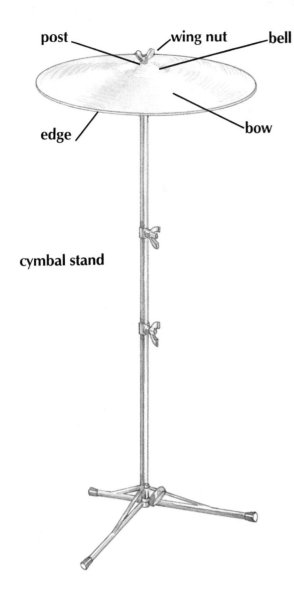

SETTING UP THE SUSPENDED CYMBAL

STEP 1
Set up the cymbal stand so that it rests solidly on the floor.

STEP 2
Adjust the stand so that the cymbal will be at waist height and parallel to the floor.

STEP 3
Place the cymbal on the cymbal stand. Be sure that the felt washer and rubber post insulator prevent the cymbal from coming in contact with any metal part of the stand.

STEP 4
Attach the wing nut to the post. Do not overtighten the wing nut.

PLAYING THE SUSPENDED CYMBAL

STEP 1
Hold a drum stick or yarn mallet using the same grip you use when playing mallet percussion instruments.

STEP 2
Using a full wrist stroke, strike the cymbal on the bow with the end of the stick or mallet. Use a quick down-up motion.

STEP 3
When striking the suspended cymbal, imagine that you are drawing the tone out of the cymbal.

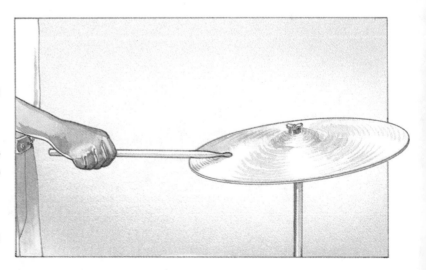

The Triangle (Tri.)

Preparing To Play

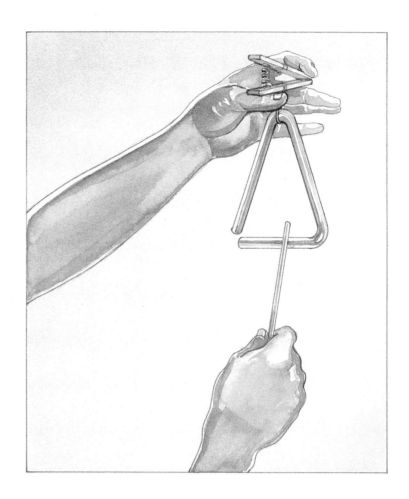

STEP 1
With your left hand, grasp the clip attached to the triangle.

STEP 2
With your right hand, hold the triangle beater between your thumb and index finger.

STEP 3
Suspend the triangle in the air at shoulder height. The open end of the triangle should be to your left.

STEP 4
Position yourself and the triangle so that you can see the conductor, the triangle, and your music.

Playing The Triangle

STEP 1
Strike the triangle with a light, quick wrist motion. Strike either the outside right hand corner near the top (△) or the inside right hand corner of the base (△).

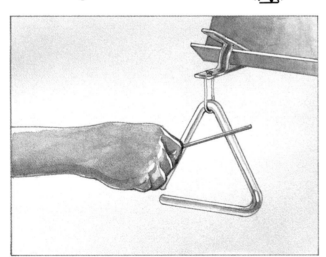

STEP 2
In certain situations, you will be required to play the triangle while it is suspended from a music stand.

STEP 3
When not being played, suspend the triangle from a music stand or rest it on a soft surface.

FOR PERCUSSION ONLY

PERCUSSION CLEF	‖	TIME SIGNATURE	$\frac{4}{4}$	QUARTER NOTE	♩	QUARTER REST	𝄽

$\frac{4}{4}$ = 4 counts in each measure

Measures

Staff

Bar Lines

Each quarter note gets 1 count in $\frac{4}{4}$ time.

Each quarter rest gets 1 count in $\frac{4}{4}$ time.

STICKING

L = left hand   R = right hand

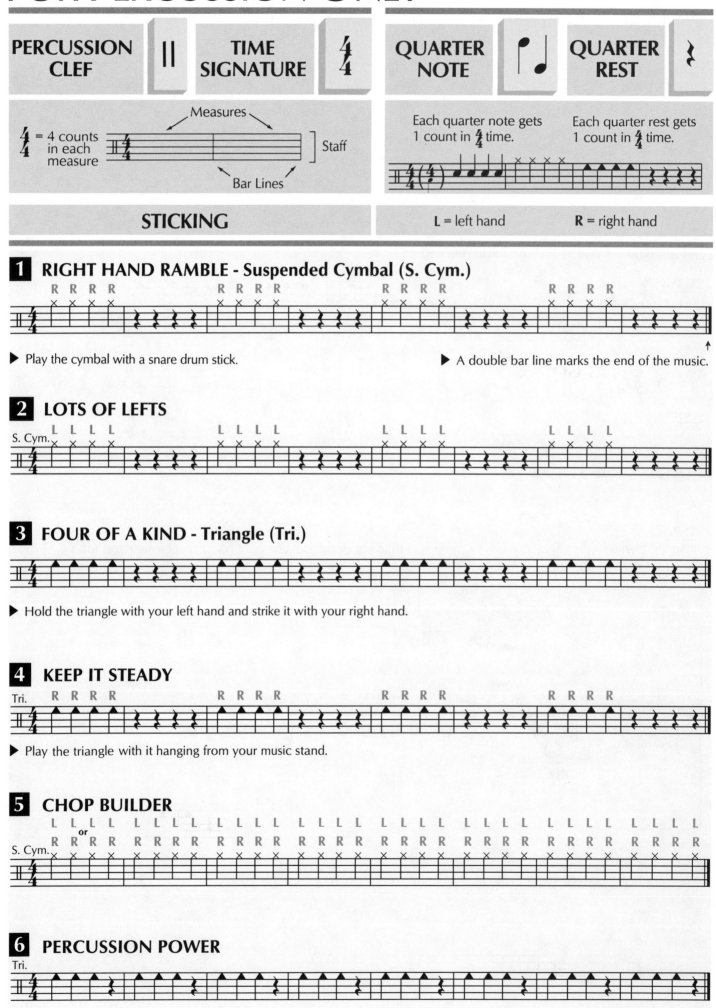

1 RIGHT HAND RAMBLE - Suspended Cymbal (S. Cym.)

▶ Play the cymbal with a snare drum stick.

▶ A double bar line marks the end of the music.

2 LOTS OF LEFTS

3 FOUR OF A KIND - Triangle (Tri.)

▶ Hold the triangle with your left hand and strike it with your right hand.

4 KEEP IT STEADY

▶ Play the triangle with it hanging from your music stand.

5 CHOP BUILDER

6 PERCUSSION POWER

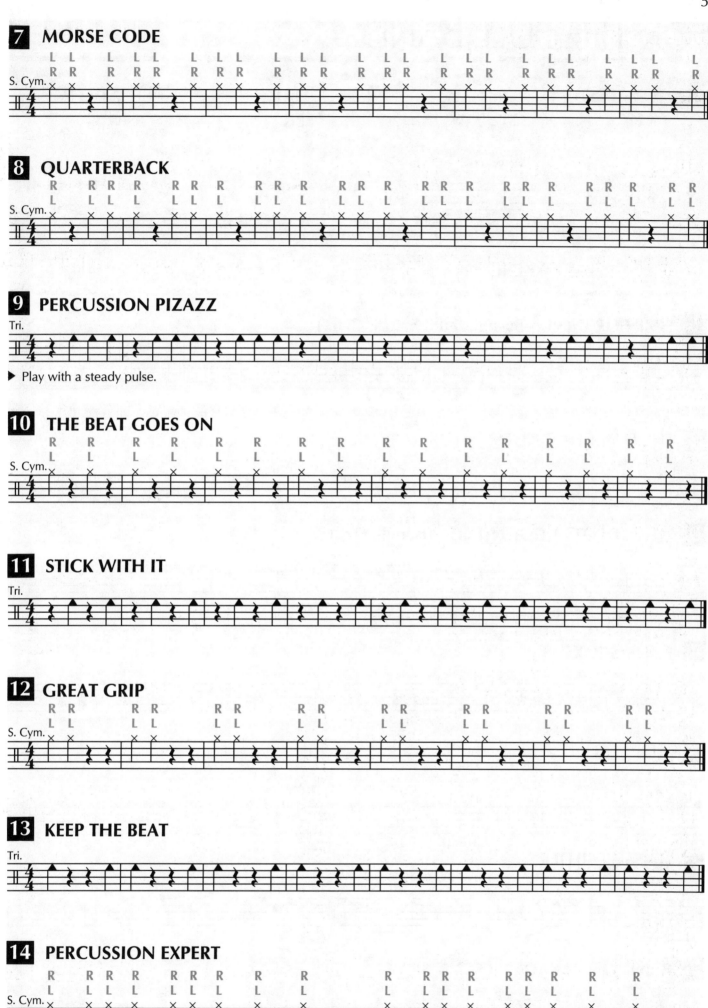

7 MORSE CODE

8 QUARTERBACK

9 PERCUSSION PIZAZZ

▶ Play with a steady pulse.

10 THE BEAT GOES ON

11 STICK WITH IT

12 GREAT GRIP

13 KEEP THE BEAT

14 PERCUSSION EXPERT

FOR THE FULL BAND

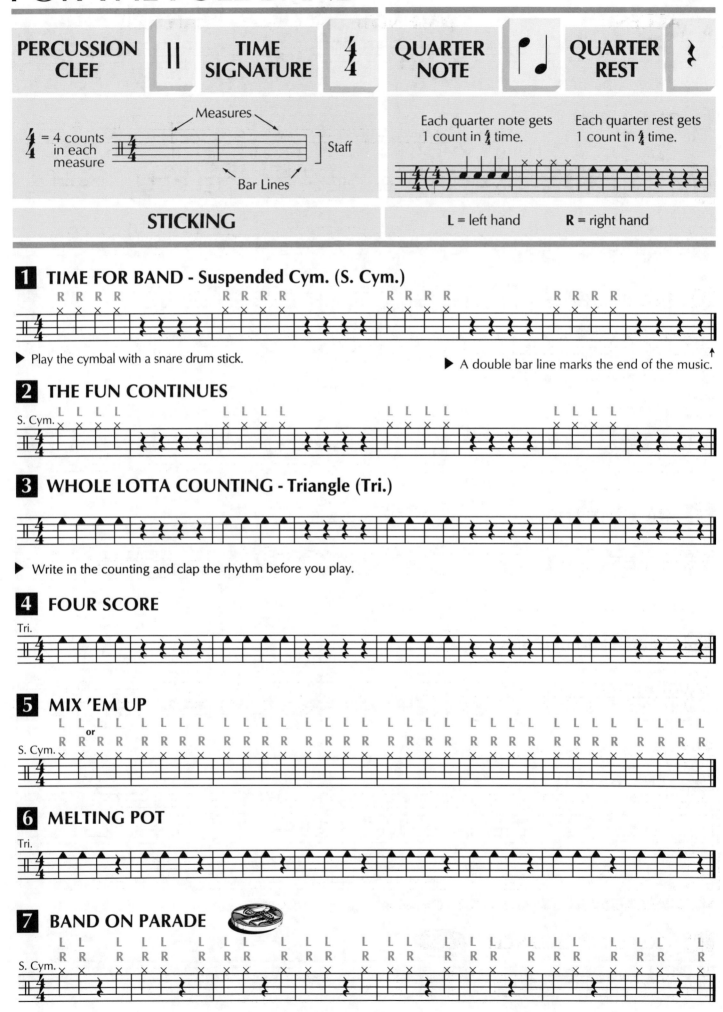

> Lines with a medal are *Achievement Lines*. The chart on page 47 can be used to record your progress.

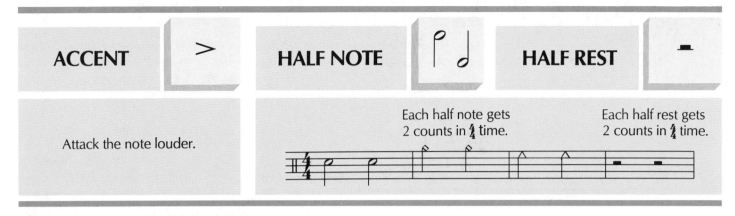

8 A BREATH OF FRESH AIR

9 SIDE BY SIDE

10 TWO BY TWO

11 HALF THE PRICE

▶ Write in the counting and clap the rhythm before you play.

12 CARDIFF BY THE SEA

Welsh Folk Song

13 TWO FOR THE SHOW - Duet

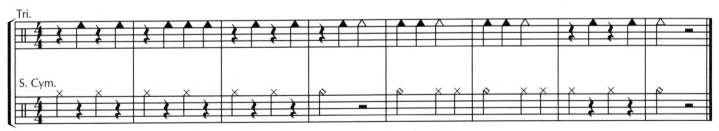

▶ One percussionist should play the Tri. while another percussionist plays the S. Cym.

14 GO FOR EXCELLENCE!

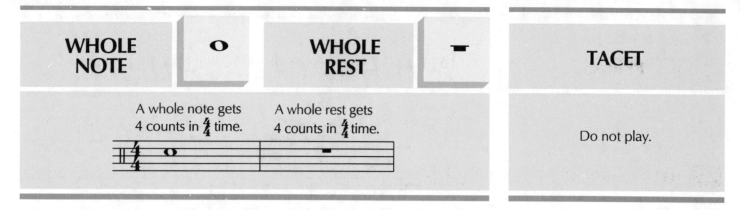

WHOLE NOTE	o	WHOLE REST	▬	TACET
A whole note gets 4 counts in $\frac{4}{4}$ time.		A whole rest gets 4 counts in $\frac{4}{4}$ time.		Do not play.

THE WOOD BLOCK (W. Blk.)

PLAYING THE WOOD BLOCK

STEP 1
Hold the bottom of the wood block with one hand. Do not squeeze the wood block too tightly.

STEP 2
In your other hand, hold a drum stick or hard rubber mallet. Use the same grip you use when playing mallet percussion instruments.

STEP 3
Strike the wood block in the center of the top part. Use a quick down-up wrist motion.

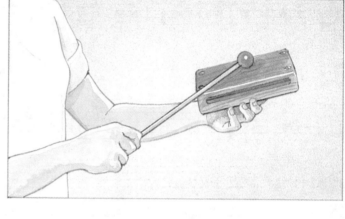

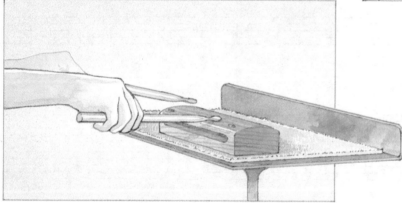

STEP 4
When playing fast wood block parts, place the wood block on a soft, flat surface, and use two mallets or sticks.

15 **A QUARTER'S WORTH - Wood Block (W. Blk.)**

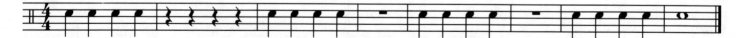

▶ Write in the counting and clap the rhythm before you play.

16 **HOT CROSS BUNS - Tacet**

PHRASE

A phrase is a musical thought or sentence.
Phrases are usually four or eight measures long.

17 AU CLAIRE DE LA LUNE

French Folk Song

W. Blk.

▶ Draw in a breath mark (') at the end of each phrase.

18 DOWN BY THE STATION

Traditional

W. Blk.

19 EASY STREET

S. Cym.

20 COUNTRY WALK

English Folk Song

Tri.

21 GETTIN' IT TOGETHER

W. Blk.

22 FOR PERCUSSION ONLY

S. Cym.

Tri.

▶ For a challenge, one person may play both parts. To do this, play the S. Cym. with your left hand and the Tri. with your right hand.

9

REPEAT SIGN	COMMON TIME	FERMATA

Repeat from the beginning.

$\mathbf{C} = \frac{4}{4}$
Common time means the same as $\frac{4}{4}$ time.

Hold the note or rest longer than its usual value.

23 MERRILY WE ROLL ALONG   Traditional

▶ Play this exercise with your right hand the first time through and with your left hand the second time through.

24 LIGHTLY ROW - Duet   Traditional

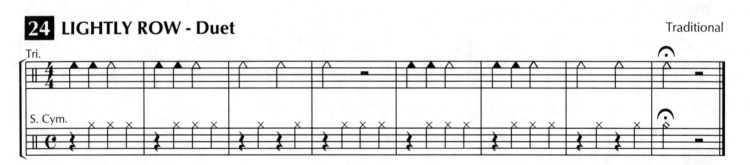

▶ Are you striking the correct part of the triangle? Are you striking the cymbal on the bow with the tip of your stick?

25 ONE STEP AT A TIME

▶ Write in the counting and clap the rhythm before you play.

SOLO	One person plays.	**SOLI**	Whole section plays.	**TUTTI**	Everyone plays.

THE SLEIGH BELLS (S.B.)

PLAYING THE SLEIGH BELLS

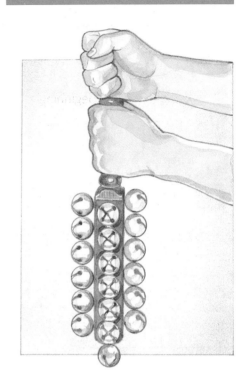

STEP 1
Hold the handle of the sleigh bells in one hand, with the bells pointing toward the floor.

STEP 2
Make a fist with your other hand and firmly hit the upper end of the sleigh bells.

26 **GOOD KING WENCESLAS - Sleigh Bells (S.B.)**   Traditional English Carol

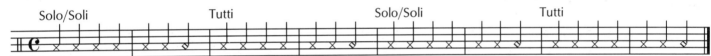

▶ Are you holding and striking the sleigh bells correctly?

27 **SONG OF THE FJORDS**   Norwegian Folk Song

▶ Use a larger stroke when playing the accented notes.

28 _____   Composer _____
                                                                                          your name

▶ Fill in the rest of the measures using rhythms you know. Make sure there are four counts in each measure. Title and play your composition.

29 **GO FOR EXCELLENCE!**

10

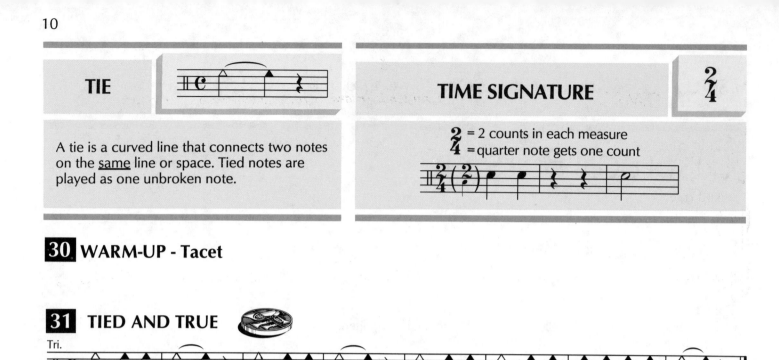

30 WARM-UP - Tacet

31 TIED AND TRUE

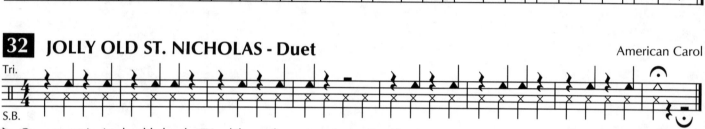

32 JOLLY OLD ST. NICHOLAS - Duet

American Carol

▶ One percussionist should play the Tri. while another percussionist plays the S.B.

33 AMIGOS

Mexican Folk Song

▶ Keep on playing!

▶ Write in the counting and clap the rhythm before you play.

34 FARM OUT

Traditional

35 FOR SUSPENDED CYMBAL ONLY

THE TAMBOURINE (Tamb.)

PLAYING THE TAMBOURINE

STEP 1
Hold the tambourine at chest level with one hand. Your thumb should be on the "head side" with your other fingers underneath. The head should be at an angle to the floor.

STEP 2
Strike the tambourine near the edge with the first three fingers of your other hand. Use a quick wrist motion, keeping your fingers on the head after making contact.

STEP 3
When you practice, sometimes hold the tambourine in your right hand and strike it with your left. Other times, hold the tambourine in your left hand and strike it with your right.

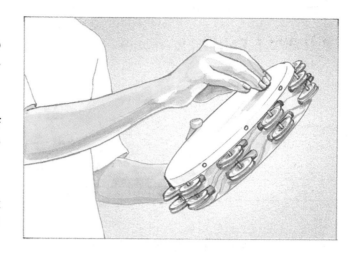

36 MARK TIME - Tacet

37 SWEETLY SINGS THE DONKEY - Tacet

38 MARY ANN - Tambourine (Tamb.)

West Indies Folk Song

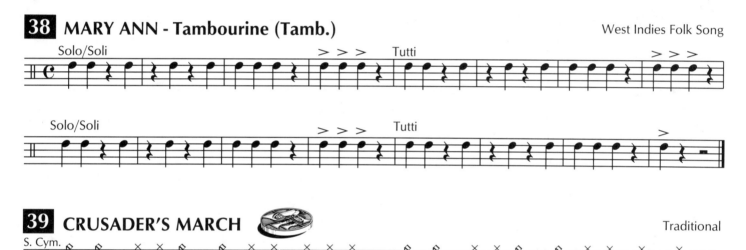

39 CRUSADER'S MARCH

Traditional

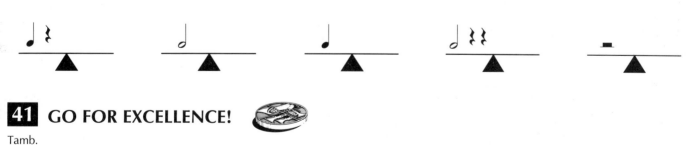

▶ Write in the counting and clap the rhythm before you play.

40 BALANCE THE SCALES

Draw *one* note or *one* rest to balance each scale.

41 GO FOR EXCELLENCE!

Tamb.

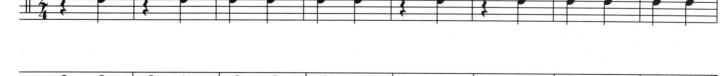

W21TM

ONE-MEASURE REPEAT SIGN

Repeat the previous measure.

BALANCE BUILDER - Tacet

Suspended Cymbal
Wood Block
Sleigh Bells

JINGLE BELLS
Band Arrangement

J. S. Pierpont (1822 - 1893)
arr. Chuck Elledge (b. 1961)

42 SCHOOL SONG

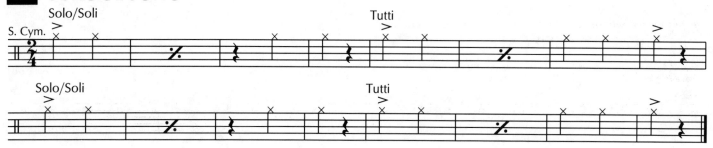

43 FOR WOOD BLOCK ONLY

▶ Place the W. Blk. on a percussion table. Play the W. Blk. using two mallets.

EIGHTH NOTES

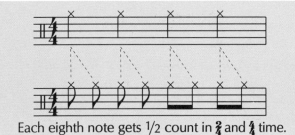

Each eighth note gets ½ count in ⅔ and ⁴⁄₄ time.

Two eighth notes are as long as a quarter note.

½ + ½ = 1 count

44 **WARM-UP - Tacet**

45 **EIGHTH NOTE ENCOUNTER**

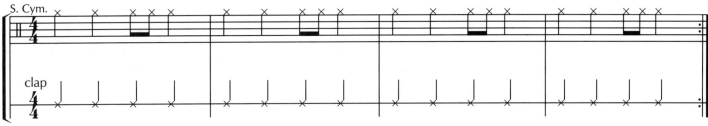

▶ Write in the counting for the top line before you play.

46 **JIM ALONG JOSIE**

American Folk Song

▶ Use two mallets.

47 **EIGHTH NOTE EXPLORER**

▶ Write in the counting for the top line before you play.

48 **GO TELL BILL**

Gioacchino Rossini (1792 - 1868)

49 **GO FOR EXCELLENCE!**

50 EIGHTH NOTE EXPRESS

Tamb.

clap

▶ Write in the counting for the top line before you play.

51 SKIP IT, LOU

American Folk Song

W. Blk.   Solo/Soli   Tutti

Solo/Soli   Tutti

52 EIGHTH NOTE EXPERT

S. Cym.

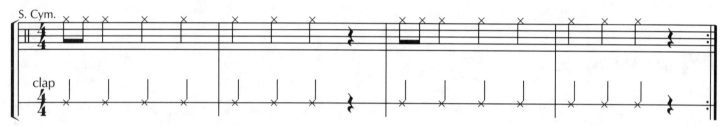

clap

▶ Write in the counting for the top line before you play.

53 MEXICAN MOUNTAIN SONG

Mexican Folk Song

Tamb.

54 BAFFLING BAR LINES

S.B.

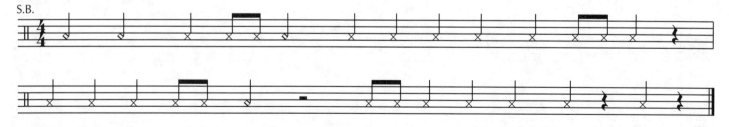

▶ Write in the counting and draw in the bar lines before you play.

55 FOR WOOD BLOCK ONLY

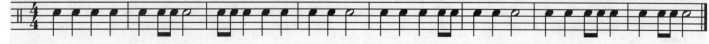

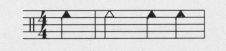

PICK-UP NOTE — A note that comes before the first full measure of a piece of music.

56 WARM-UP - Tacet

57 THEME FROM "SYMPHONY NO. 1"   Johannes Brahms (1833 - 1897)

58 ERIE CANAL CAPERS   American Work Song

59 LAUGHING SONG - Round   Traditional

60 STAR SEARCH   Wolfgang Amadeus Mozart (1756 - 1791)

61 GO FOR EXCELLENCE!

▶ For a challenge, one person may play both parts. To do this, play the W. Blk. with your left hand and the S. Cym. with your right hand.

W21TM

THE TIMPANI (Timp.)

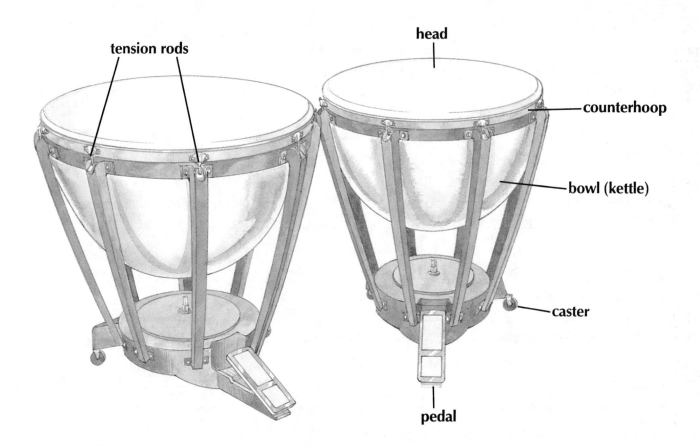

tension rods

head

counterhoop

bowl (kettle)

caster

pedal

TIMPANI MALLET

PREPARING TO PLAY

STEP 1
Set up the timpani with the large drum to the left and the pedals directly in front of you.

STEP 2
Position your music stand so that you can see the conductor and your music at the same time.

STEP 3
Stand in a comfortable position eight to twelve inches from the drums with your feet slightly spread and your weight distributed evenly on both feet.

STEP 4
Hold the timpani mallets using the same grip you use when playing mallet percussion instruments.

PLAYING THE TIMPANI

STEP 1
Using a quick wrist snap, strike the drum approximately three to four inches from the edge of the bowl.

STEP 2
Always use a <u>full, relaxed stroke</u> on the timpani. Allow the mallet to rebound naturally back to the position (height) from which it started.

STEP 3
When playing timpani, always remain relaxed. Imagine that you are drawing the tone out of the drums.

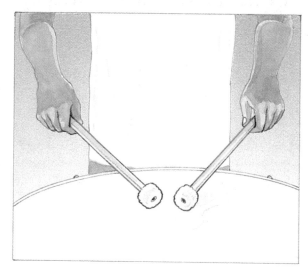

TUNING THE TIMPANI

STEP 1
Place your foot on the pedal. Be sure that the pedal is set so that there is as little tension on the head as possible.

STEP 2
Play the desired note using a pitch pipe.

STEP 3
Listen carefully to the note, then hum or sing it to yourself.

STEP 4
Strike the head once with the mallet. While the drum is still ringing, press down on the pedal until the desired note is reached.

STEP 5
Hum or sing the desired note again and check the tuning by tapping the head. If the pitch of the drum is below the note you are singing, keep increasing the tension until the desired note is reached. If the pitch of the drum is higher than the note you are singing, release all the tension and begin again with STEP 2.

CARING FOR THE TIMPANI

STEP 1
If the heads are plastic, clean them regularly with a damp cloth.

STEP 2
Replace the heads when they become worn, dented, or punctured.

STEP 3
Always be sure that head protectors are placed on the timpani after you are finished playing them.

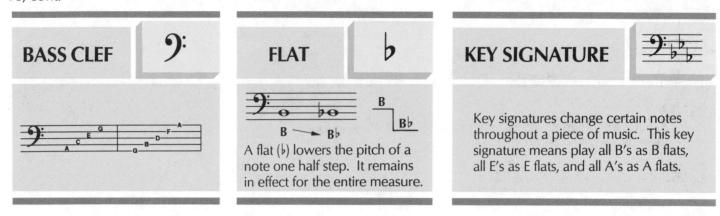

BASS CLEF

FLAT

A flat (♭) lowers the pitch of a note one half step. It remains in effect for the entire measure.

KEY SIGNATURE

Key signatures change certain notes throughout a piece of music. This key signature means play all B's as B flats, all E's as E flats, and all A's as A flats.

---

62 CLIMBING STAIRS - Timpani (Timp.)   Page 41 ▮▮▮▮➤

▶ When you see a page number followed by an arrow, *Excellerate* to the page indicated for additional studies.

---

63 BINGO

American Folk Song

▶ Percussion parts can appear on any line or space.

---

64 THERE'S MUSIC IN THE AIR

George F. Root (1820 - 1895)

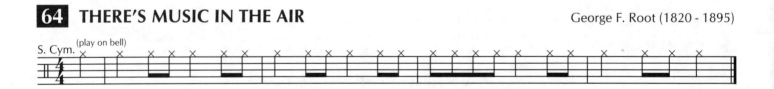

---

65 THERE'S THE SAME MUSIC IN THE AIR - Tacet

---

66 SCALE SKILL - Tacet

---

67 FOR TIMPANI ONLY

▶ Circle the notes changed by the key signature.

KEY SIGNATURE

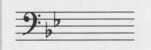

This key signature means play all B's as B flats and all E's as E flats.

DOTTED HALF NOTE

A dot after a note adds half the value of the note.

♩ + • = ♩ + ♩ = ♩.
2 + 1 = 2 + 1 = 3 counts

TIME SIGNATURE

3/4 = 3 counts in each measure
= quarter note gets 1 count

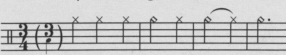

DYNAMICS

forte (*f*) - loud

piano (*p*) - soft

68 **WARM-UP**   Page 41 ▦▶

69 **CHANNEL THREE**

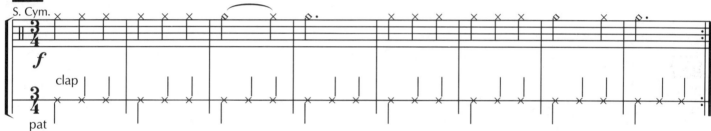

▶ Write in the counting for the top line before you play.

70 **DOWN IN THE VALLEY**

American Mountain Song

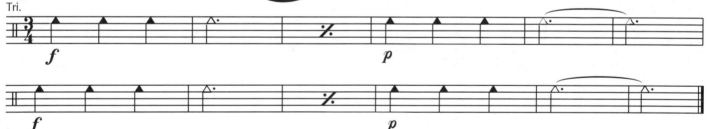

71 **BROTHER MARTIN - Round - Tacet**

72 **THE LITTLE FISH**

Australian Folk Song

▶ Draw in a breath mark at the end of each phrase.

73 **GO FOR EXCELLENCE!**

Czech Folk Song

"When Love Is Kind"

W21TM

18

74 WARM-UP

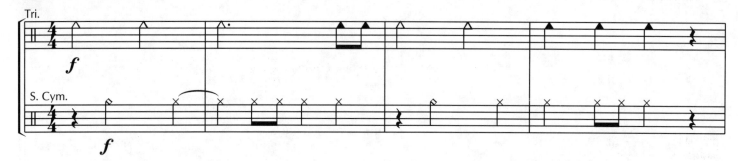

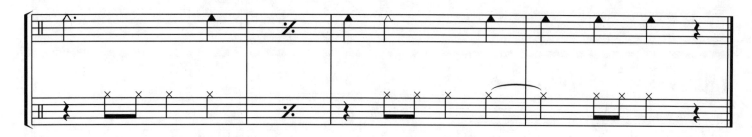

75 OLD BLUE

Traditional

76 THIRD TIME AROUND

▶ Are you holding and striking the sleigh bells correctly?

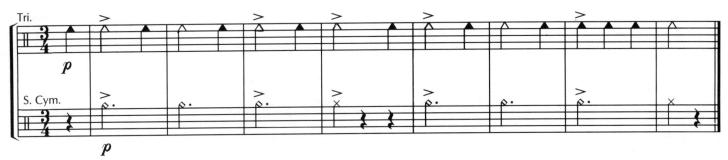

| SINGLE EIGHTH NOTE | ♪ ♪ | EIGHTH REST | ♪ |

Each eighth note and eighth rest gets 1/2 count in $\frac{2}{4}$, $\frac{3}{4}$, and $\frac{4}{4}$ time.

77 LULLABY - Duet

Traditional

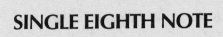

▶ Play the S. Cym. on the bow, using a yarn mallet. On the rests, stop the S. Cym. from ringing with your free hand. This is called *dampening*.

78 MINUTEMAN MARCH

Robert Frost (b. 1942)

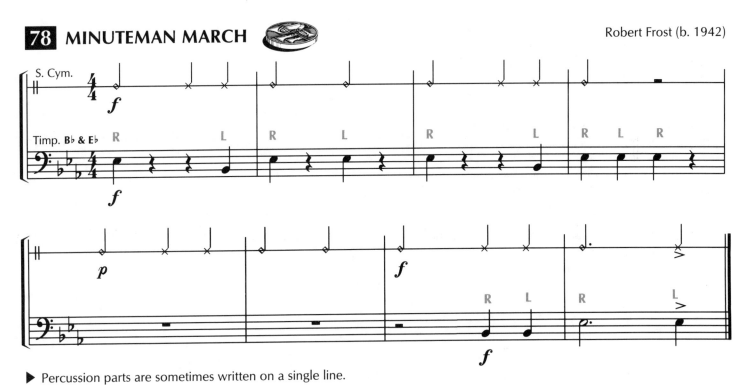

▶ Percussion parts are sometimes written on a single line.

79 FOR TIMPANI ONLY

▶ When the sticking is in parentheses, move the stick but do not strike the drum head.

1st and 2nd ENDINGS	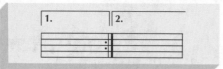	Play the first ending the first time through. Then, repeat the music, skip the first ending, and play the second ending.

THE CLAVES

PLAYING THE CLAVES

STEP 1
Cup one hand. Place one of the claves on it so that the clave rests between the base of your thumb and the ends of your fingers. Your hand should form a hollow chamber underneath the clave.

STEP 2
Hold the other clave by the end in your other hand.

STEP 3
Hold your cupped hand motionless, and bring the clave you are holding by the end down to strike the clave on your cupped hand.

STEP 4
Practice playing the claves with the roles of your hands reversed.

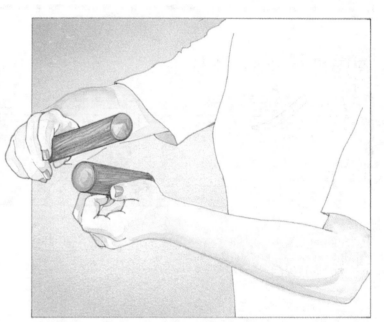

THE MARACAS (Marc.)

PLAYING THE MARACAS

STEP 1
Hold one maraca in each hand. Grasp the handle of each with your thumb and three smallest fingers. Extend your index finger so that it touches the shell.

STEP 2
Using your wrist, flick one of the maracas. This causes the beads inside the maraca to hit against the inside wall of the shell, creating a "tsk" sound.

STEP 3
To play consecutive notes, first flick one maraca, and then the other. The motion will be similar to the motion used to play alternating strokes on the snare drum.

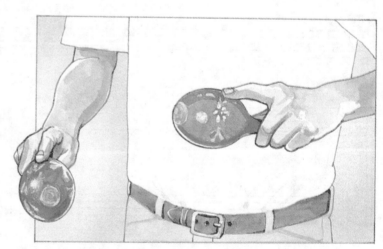

80 MEXICAN HAT DANCE - Maracas (Marc.) & Claves　　　Mexican Folk Song

81 FRÈRE JACQUES - Tacet

82 MORNING MOOD

Edvard Grieg (1843 - 1907)

83 MING COURT

Chinese Folk Song

84 GO FOR EXCELLENCE!

SAWMILL CREEK
Percussion Solo or Ensemble

Bruce Pearson (b. 1942)

Suspended Cymbal
Tambourine

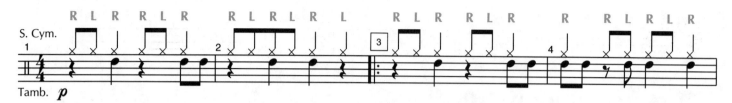

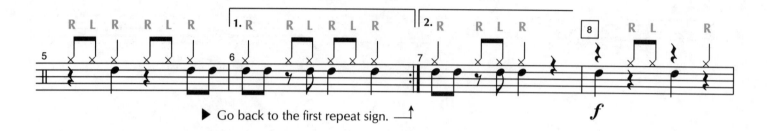

▶ Go back to the first repeat sign. ⟶

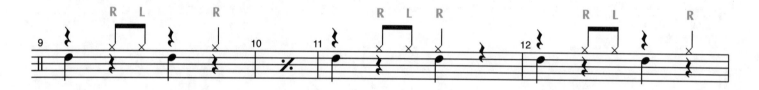

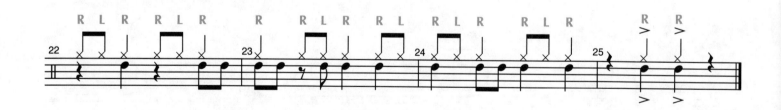

Timpani

SAWMILL CREEK
Percussion Solo or Ensemble

Bruce Pearson (b. 1942)

► Go back to the first repeat sign. ⟶

MONTEGO BAY
Band Arrangement

Calypso Song
arr. Chuck Elledge (b. 1961)

Suspended Cymbal
Maracas
Claves

MONTEGO BAY
Band Arrangement

Timpani

Calypso Song
arr. Chuck Elledge (b. 1961)

▶ Use a larger stroke when playing the accented notes.

LONG REST

Count: 1 2 3 4 2 2 3 4

Rest the number of measures indicated.

Suspended Cymbal
Triangle

REGAL MARCH
Band Arrangement

Bruce Pearson (b. 1942)
arr. Chuck Elledge (b. 1961)

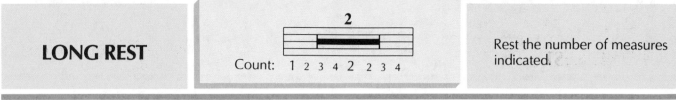

LONG REST

2

Count: 1 2 3 4 2 2 3 4

Rest the number of measures indicated.

REGAL MARCH
Band Arrangement

Timpani

Bruce Pearson (b. 1942)
arr. Chuck Elledge (b. 1961)

▶ Use a larger stroke when playing the accented notes.

ROLL

A roll may be used to sustain the sound on a percussion instrument.

PLAYING A SUSPENDED CYMBAL ROLL

STEP 1
Hold a yarn mallet in each hand using your normal grip.

STEP 2
Position the mallets opposite each other over the bow of the cymbal.

STEP 3
Using your wrists, create the roll by playing alternating single strokes on the cymbal. Alternate only as fast as necessary to sustain the sound of the cymbal. Striking the cymbal too often may deaden the sound.

STEP 4
Always use relaxed strokes to ensure a full, sustained sound.

85 WARM-UP

▶ Dampen the S. Cym. on the rests by grasping the cymbal with one or both hands.

86 FULL OF HOT AIR

▶ Use slow, relaxed strokes when playing soft S. Cym. rolls.

87 DANZA GIOVANNI

Italian Folk Song

88 B♭ MAJOR SCALE SKILL Page 41 ▶

▶ Carefully observe the indicated stickings.

89 THE MAN ON THE FLYING TRAPEZE

George Leybourne (1842 - 1884)

▶ Go back to the first repeat sign. ⤴

90 _____ Composer _____
your name

▶ Using the given rhythms, draw in notes to complete the song. Title and play your composition.

91 FOR TIMPANI ONLY

▶ Are you using even, relaxed strokes?

THE TEMPLE BLOCKS (T. Blks.)

PLAYING THE TEMPLE BLOCKS

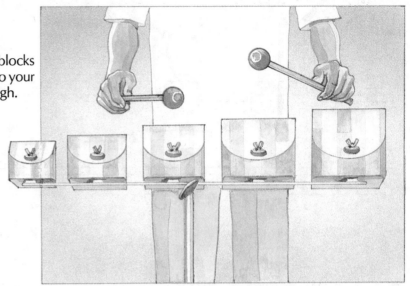

STEP 1
Set up the instrument with the largest (lowest pitched) blocks to your left, and the smallest (highest pitched) blocks to your right. Adjust the stand so that the blocks are waist high.

STEP 2
Stand in a comfortable position behind the temple blocks with your feet slightly spread and your weight distributed evenly on both feet.

STEP 3
Hold a rubber mallet in each hand using your normal grip.

STEP 4
Strike the blocks on the top center of each block, using the same down-up wrist motion you use when playing wood block or mallet percussion instruments.

92 LOOK SHARP - Temple Blocks (T. Blks.)

▶ Play the high block with your right hand and the low block with your left hand. Experiment with different pairs of blocks.

93 AURA LEE

G. R. Poulton (d. 1867)

▶ Are you holding the maracas correctly?

94 BARCAROLLE

Jacques Offenbach (1819 - 1880)

KEY SIGNATURE

This key signature means play all B's as B flats.

95 JUST BY ACCIDENT

96 F MAJOR SCALE SKILL

97 SAILOR'S SONG

98 GO FOR EXCELLENCE!

American Folk Song

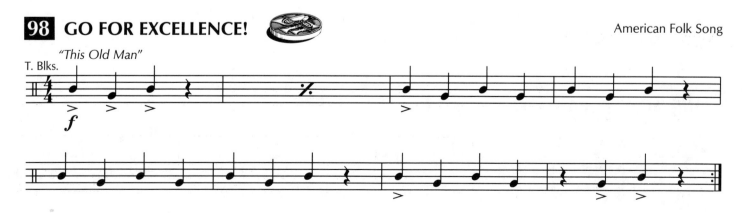

DA CAPO AL FINE (D. C. AL FINE)	Go back to the beginning and play until the *Fine*.

PLAYING A TRIANGLE ROLL

STEP 1
Hold the triangle and triangle beater as you would normally.

STEP 2
Suspend the triangle with the open end of the triangle to your left. Position yourself and the triangle so that you can see the conductor, the triangle, and your music.

STEP 3
Using your wrist, create the roll by quickly moving the beater back and forth at either connected corner of the triangle. The beater should strike the sides of the triangle as it moves back and forth.

STEP 4
In certain situations, you will be required to play a triangle roll while the triangle is suspended from a music stand.

99 WARM-UP - Tacet   **100** IN THE POCKET - Tacet

101 POCKET CHANGE - Tacet   **102** STRICTLY BUSINESS - Tacet

103 SMOOTH SAILING

104 ROSES FROM THE SOUTH — Johann Strauss, Jr. (1825 - 1899)

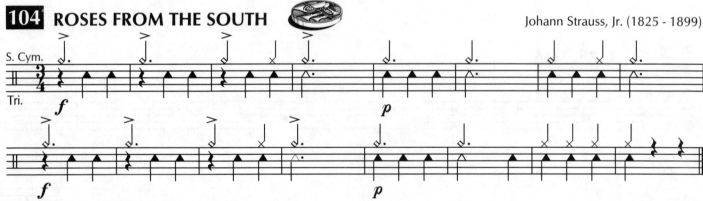

105 THEME FROM "HANSEL AND GRETEL" — Engelbert Humperdinck (1854 - 1921) *D.C. al Fine*

106 FOR TIMPANI ONLY — Page 41

107 THAT'S A WRAP

108 POLLY WOLLY DOODLE
American Folk Song

109 VOLGA BOAT SONG
Russian Folk Song

▶ Remember to dampen the S. Cym. on the rest.

110 KOOKABURRA - Round
Australian Folk Song

111 GO FOR EXCELLENCE!
Tielman Susato (1500? - 1561?)
"Ronde"

DOTTED QUARTER NOTE

A dot after a note adds half the value of the note.

$$\quarternote + \cdot = \quarternote + \eighthnote = \dottedquarternote$$
$$1 + \tfrac{1}{2} = 1 + \tfrac{1}{2} = 1\ \tfrac{1}{2}\ \text{counts}$$

112 WARM-UP - Band Arrangement

113 SHORT CUT

▶ Write in the counting for the top line before you play.

114 SPOT THE DOTS

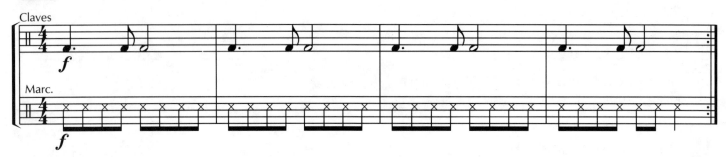

▶ Feel the pulse of three eighth notes during each dotted quarter note.

115 ALL THROUGH THE NIGHT

Welsh Folk Song

116 ALOUETTE

French–Canadian Folk Song

THE CRASH CYMBALS (C. Cyms.)

PREPARING TO PLAY

STEP 1
Stand up straight with your feet slightly spread and your weight distributed evenly on both feet.

STEP 2
Grip the strap of either cymbal between your index finger and thumb. Grip close to the cymbal bell. For a better cymbal sound, remove any pads on the outside of the cymbals.

STEP 3
Curl the rest of your fingers around the strap, squeezing the whole strap firmly. Your thumb may rest against the bell to help control the movement of the cymbal.

STEP 4
Repeat STEPS 2 and 3 with your other hand. If the crash cymbals you are using have wood or plastic handles rather than flexible straps, grasp the handles firmly in each hand.

PLAYING THE CRASH CYMBALS

STEP 1
Hold the cymbals at an angle, with the edge of the right cymbal lower than the edge of the left.

STEP 2
Without moving the left cymbal, bring the right cymbal inward and upward, and strike against the left cymbal with a glancing motion.

STEP 3
If repeated strokes are necessary, return to the starting position and continue with STEP 2.

STEP 4
If no additional strokes are necessary for several counts, bring both cymbals to an open position.

STEP 5
To dampen the ringing of the cymbals, firmly pull the edges of the cymbals in against your upper arms, chest, or mid-body.

117 FOR CRASH CYMBALS (C. Cyms.) ONLY

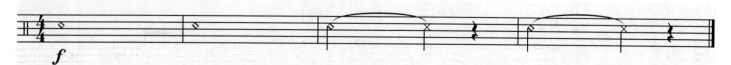

f

TWO-MEASURE REPEAT SIGN

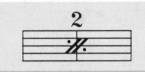

Repeat the two previous measures.

118 JUST A LITTLE OFF THE TOP

▶ When playing the C. Cyms., experiment with different angles and distances between the cymbals.

119 TOP DRAWER - Duet

120 HOME ON THE RANGE

Daniel E. Kelley (1843 - 1905)

▶ Circle the notes changed by the key signature.

PLAYING A TIMPANI ROLL

STEP 1
Hold the timpani mallets using your normal grip.

STEP 2
Create the roll by playing alternating single strokes on the drum. Remain relaxed. Always use full, even strokes.

STEP 3
Let the natural vibrations of the head create the sustained sound.   In general, the lower the drum is tuned, the slower the roll strokes need to be. Drums tuned to higher pitches usually require faster roll strokes.

121 **THE CONQUERING HERO - Duet** Page 41 George Frideric Handel (1685 - 1759)

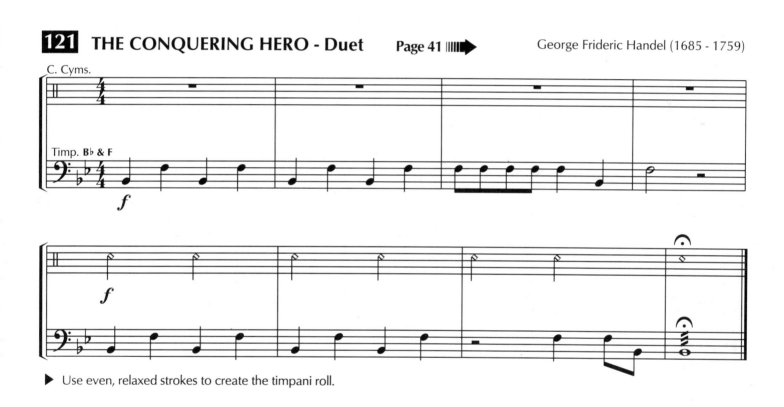

▶ Use even, relaxed strokes to create the timpani roll.

122 **GO FOR EXCELLENCE!**

28

TEMPOS	**Andante** - moderately slow **Moderato** - moderate speed **Allegro** - quick and lively	DYNAMICS	*mezzo forte* (**mf**) - medium loud *mezzo piano* (**mp**) - medium soft

123 WARM-UP - Band Arrangement

Andante

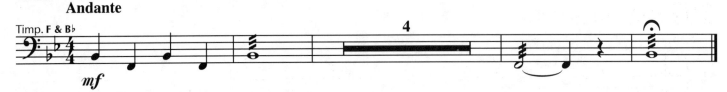

124 HIGH WINDS AHEAD

Andante

▶ Remember to dampen on the rests.

125 LOOK BEFORE YOU LEAP

Tri. Moderato

126 E♭ MAJOR SCALE SKILL

Timp. B♭ & E♭ Allegro

127 VARIATIONS ON A THEME BY MOZART

Wolfgang Amadeus Mozart (1756 – 1791)

Moderato

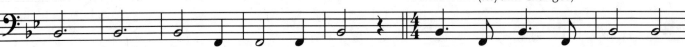

128 FOR TIMPANI ONLY

Andante

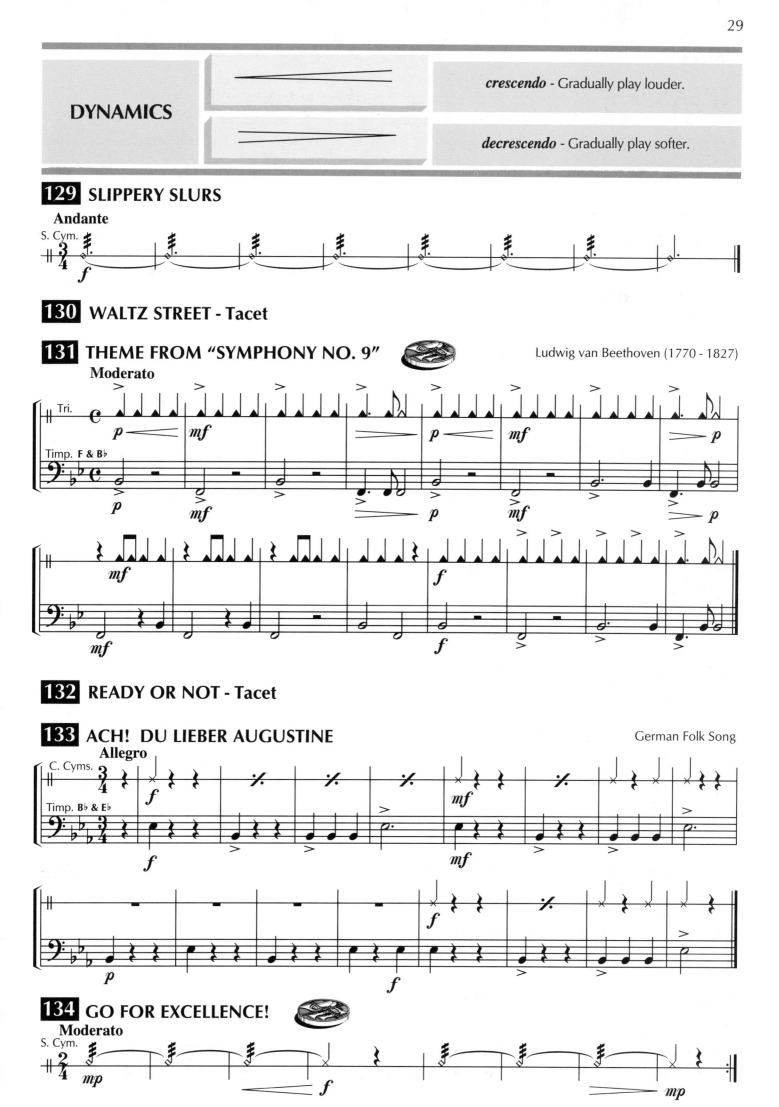

DYNAMICS

crescendo - Gradually play louder.

decrescendo - Gradually play softer.

129 SLIPPERY SLURS

Andante

130 WALTZ STREET - Tacet

131 THEME FROM "SYMPHONY NO. 9"   Ludwig van Beethoven (1770 - 1827)

Moderato

132 READY OR NOT - Tacet

133 ACH! DU LIEBER AUGUSTINE   German Folk Song

Allegro

134 GO FOR EXCELLENCE!

Moderato

BALANCE BUILDER

Triangle
Crash Cymbals

TRUMPET VOLUNTARY
Band Arrangement

Jeremiah Clarke (1674? - 1707)
arr. Bruce Pearson (b. 1942)

Timpani

TRUMPET VOLUNTARY
Band Arrangement

Jeremiah Clarke (1674? - 1707)
arr. Bruce Pearson (b. 1942)

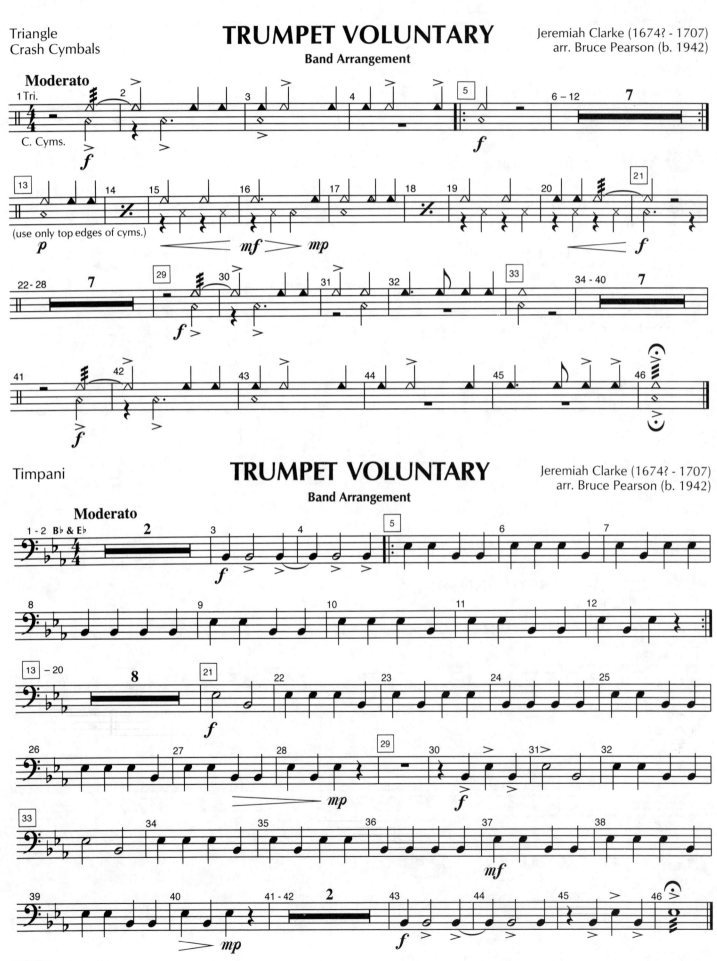

TEMPO	*Ritardando (ritard.* or *rit.)* - Gradually slow the tempo.

135 **SAKURA - Duet**   Japanese Folk Song

▶ Draw in a breath mark at the end of each phrase.

136 **GRANDFATHER'S WHISKERS**   American Folk Song

Hey!

137 **TWINKLE VARIATION**   Wolfgang Amadeus Mozart (1756 –1791)

Composer _____

your name

▶ Compose a variation on "Twinkle, Twinkle, Little Star."

138 PARTNER SONGS - Duet

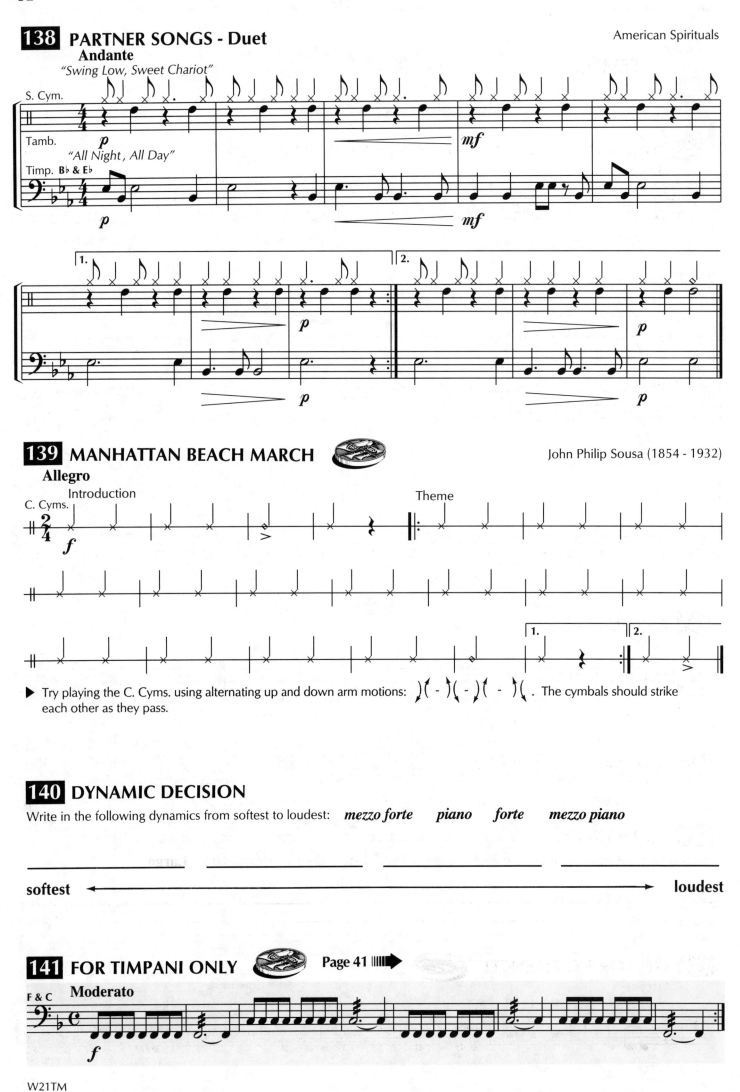

139 MANHATTAN BEACH MARCH

John Philip Sousa (1854 - 1932)

▶ Try playing the C. Cyms. using alternating up and down arm motions:)(-)(-)(-)(. The cymbals should strike each other as they pass.

140 DYNAMIC DECISION

Write in the following dynamics from softest to loudest: *mezzo forte*   *piano*   *forte*   *mezzo piano*

_____   _____   _____   _____

softest ←————————————————————————————————→ **loudest**

141 FOR TIMPANI ONLY

Page 41 ⬛⬛⬛➡

TEMPO	Largo - slow

142 "LARGO" FROM THE NEW WORLD SYMPHONY  Antonin Dvořák (1841 - 1904)

Largo

Timp. B♭ & F

mp *< mf* *> p*

143 JUST FINE

Moderato

S. Cym.

mf

Timp. F & C

R L R L R L R L R L R L R L R L R L

mf

R L R L R L R R L R L R L R L R L

144 CHORALE - Duet

Lowell Mason (1792 - 1872)

Largo

Timp. B♭ & E♭

mp < mf *mp < mf*

mp < f *mf < f > p*

rit. - - - -

145 TEMPO TIME

Write in the following tempos from slowest to fastest: **Andante Allegro Moderato Largo**

_____ _____ _____ _____

slowest ← ————————————————————→ **fastest**

146 GO FOR EXCELLENCE!

Allegro

Timp. F & C

R L R L R L R L R L L R R L R L R L R L R L R L R L L

mf

147 **RICOCHET ROCK**

Chuck Elledge (b. 1961)

148 **LOCH LOMOND**

Scottish Folk Song

149 **SHALOM, CHAVERIM**

Hebrew Folk Song

▶ Draw in a breath mark at the end of each phrase.

150 _____

Composer _____

your name

▶ Compose an ending for this song. Title and play your composition.

151 **FOR TIMPANI ONLY**

152 GRANDFATHER'S CLOCK — Henry C. Work (1832 - 1884)

153 KUM BA YAH — African Folk Song

154 GRANT US PEACE - Round — German Canon

155 GO FOR EXCELLENCE! — Page 41

ROCKIN' RONDEAU
Band Arrangement

Based on a theme by
Jean-Joseph Mouret (1682–1738)
arr. Chuck Elledge (b. 1961)

Triangle
Tambourine

ROCKIN' RONDEAU
Band Arrangement

Based on a theme by
Jean-Joseph Mouret (1682–1738)
arr. Chuck Elledge (b. 1961)

Timpani

W21TM

EXCELLERATORS - FOR TIMPANI ONLY

RHYTHM STUDIES

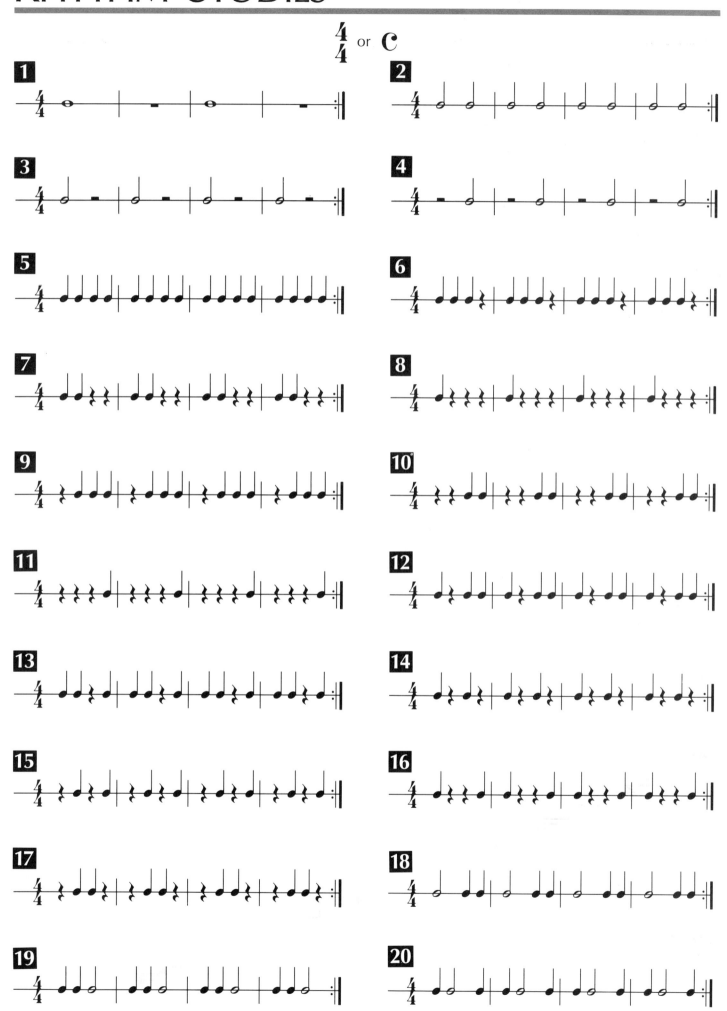

RHYTHM STUDIES

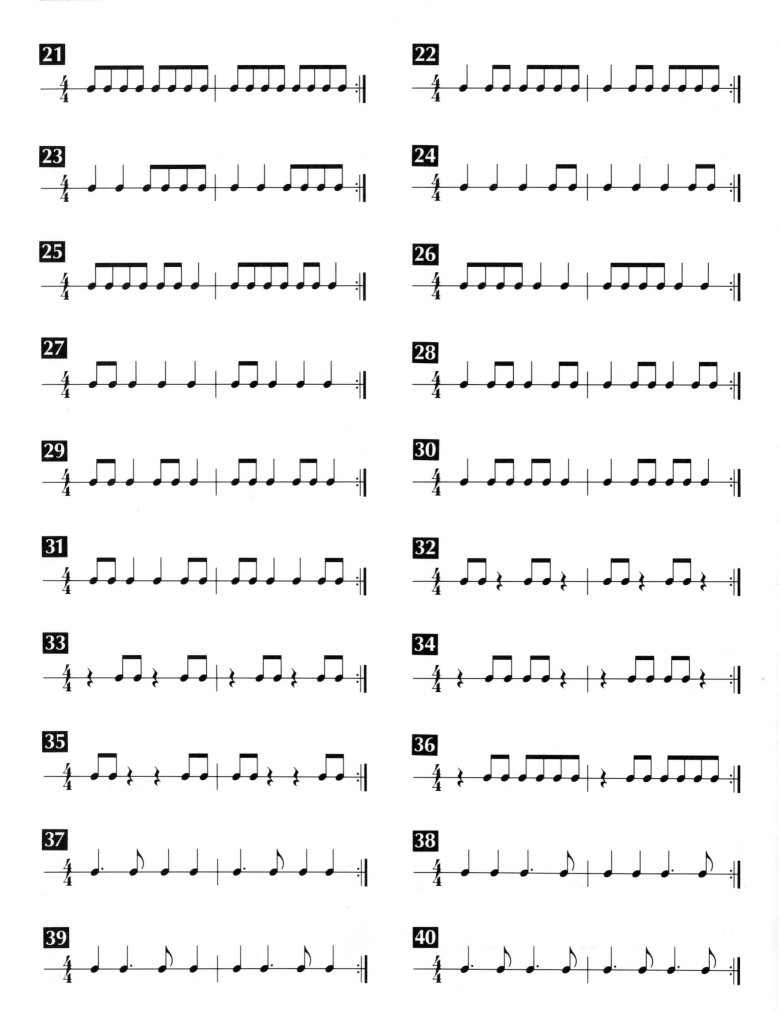

RHYTHM STUDIES

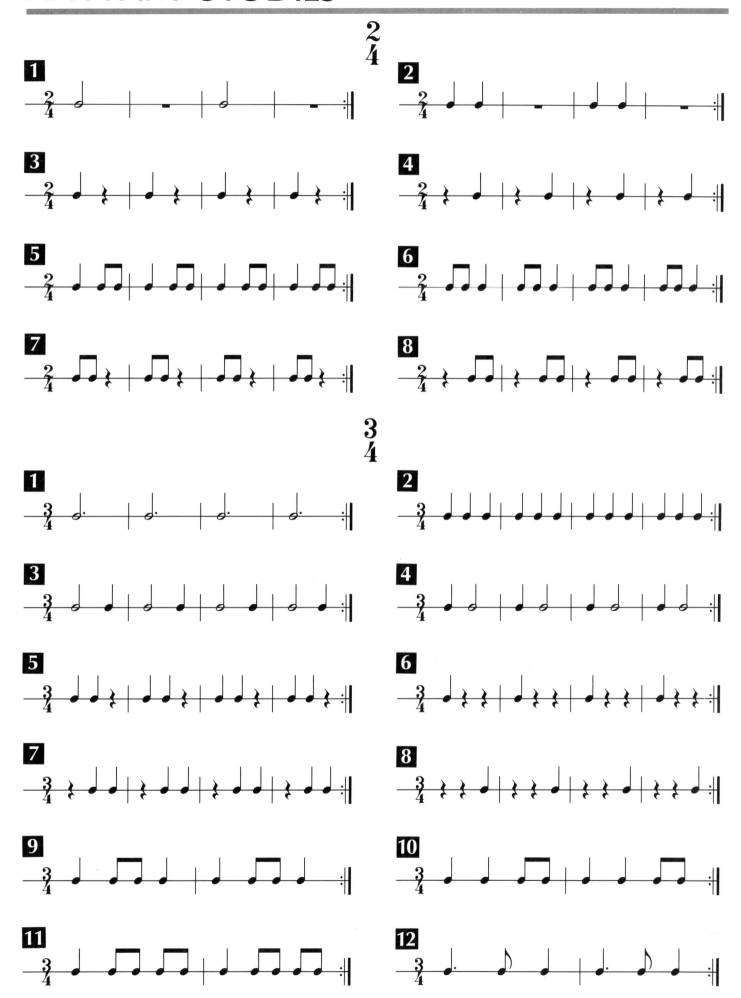

STANDARD OF EXCELLENCE

EXERCISE 7
- [ ] rhythm
- [ ] sticking
- [ ] S. Cym. tech.

EXERCISE 12
- [ ] rhythm
- [ ] accents
- [ ] S. Cym. tech.

EXERCISE 14
- [ ] rhythm
- [ ] accents
- [ ] Tri. tech.

EXERCISE 17
- [ ] rhythm
- [ ] stroke
- [ ] W. Blk. tech.

EXERCISE 22
- [ ] rhythm
- [ ] Tri. tech.
- [ ] S. Cym. tech.

EXERCISE 23
- [ ] rhythm
- [ ] repeat
- [ ] S. Cym. tech.

EXERCISE 29
- [ ] rhythm
- [ ] pulse
- [ ] S. B. tech.

EXERCISE 31
- [ ] rhythm
- [ ] pulse
- [ ] Tri. tech.

EXERCISE 35
- [ ] rhythm
- [ ] pulse
- [ ] S. Cym. tech.

EXERCISE 39
- [ ] rhythm
- [ ] stroke
- [ ] S. Cym. tech.

EXERCISE 41
- [ ] rhythm
- [ ] pulse
- [ ] Tamb. tech.

EXERCISE 43
- [ ] rhythm
- [ ] accents
- [ ] W. Blk. tech.

EXERCISE 46
- [ ] rhythm
- [ ] pulse
- [ ] W. Blk. tech.

EXERCISE 49
- [ ] rhythm
- [ ] pulse
- [ ] W. Blk. tech.

EXERCISE 53
- [ ] rhythm
- [ ] pulse
- [ ] Tamb. tech.

EXERCISE 55
- [ ] rhythm
- [ ] pulse
- [ ] W. Blk. tech.

EXERCISE 57
- [ ] rhythm
- [ ] pulse
- [ ] Tri. tech.

EXERCISE 61
- [ ] rhythm
- [ ] rhythm
- [ ] W. Blk. tech.

EXERCISE 63
- [ ] rhythm
- [ ] Tamb. tech.
- [ ] W. Blk. tech.

EXERCISE 67
- [ ] notes
- [ ] rhythm
- [ ] Timp. tech.

EXERCISE 70
- [ ] rhythm
- [ ] dynamics
- [ ] Tri. tech.

EXERCISE 73
- [ ] notes
- [ ] rhythm
- [ ] dynamics

EXERCISE 78
- [ ] notes
- [ ] rhythm
- [ ] sticking

EXERCISE 79
- [ ] notes
- [ ] rhythm
- [ ] sticking

EXERCISE 82
- [ ] notes
- [ ] rhythm
- [ ] sticking

EXERCISE 84
- [ ] rhythm
- [ ] Marc. tech.
- [ ] Claves tech.

EXERCISE 87
- [ ] notes
- [ ] rhythm
- [ ] accents

EXERCISE 91
- [ ] notes
- [ ] rhythm
- [ ] grip

EXERCISE 95
- [ ] notes
- [ ] grip
- [ ] Tri. tech.

EXERCISE 98
- [ ] rhythm
- [ ] accents
- [ ] T. Blks. tech.

EXERCISE 104
- [ ] rhythm
- [ ] S. Cym. tech.
- [ ] Tri. tech.

EXERCISE 106
- [ ] notes
- [ ] rhythm
- [ ] sticking

EXERCISE 111
- [ ] rhythm
- [ ] dynamics
- [ ] Tri. tech.

EXERCISE 115
- [ ] notes
- [ ] rhythm
- [ ] dynamics

EXERCISE 117
- [ ] rhythm
- [ ] pulse
- [ ] C. Cyms. tech.

EXERCISE 122
- [ ] rhythm
- [ ] C. Cyms. tech.
- [ ] Tri. tech.

EXERCISE 126
- [ ] rhythm
- [ ] pulse
- [ ] Timp. tech.

EXERCISE 128
- [ ] pitch
- [ ] stroke
- [ ] Timp. tech.

EXERCISE 131
- [ ] rhythm
- [ ] dynamics
- [ ] accents

EXERCISE 134
- [ ] rhythm
- [ ] dynamics
- [ ] S. Cym. tech.

EXERCISE 136
- [ ] rhythm
- [ ] rhythm
- [ ] W. Blk. tech.

EXERCISE 139
- [ ] rhythm
- [ ] rhythm
- [ ] C. Cyms. tech.

EXERCISE 141
- [ ] notes
- [ ] rhythm
- [ ] Timp. tech.

EXERCISE 142
- [ ] pitch
- [ ] rhythm
- [ ] Timp. tech.

EXERCISE 143
- [ ] rhythm
- [ ] dynamics
- [ ] Timp. tech.

EXERCISE 146
- [ ] pitch
- [ ] rhythm
- [ ] sticking

EXERCISE 148
- [ ] pitch
- [ ] rhythm
- [ ] Timp. tech.

EXERCISE 151
- [ ] pitch
- [ ] rhythm
- [ ] Timp. tech.

EXERCISE 153
- [ ] pitch
- [ ] rhythm
- [ ] sticking

EXERCISE 155
- [ ] pitch
- [ ] rhythm
- [ ] dynamics

EXCELLENCE